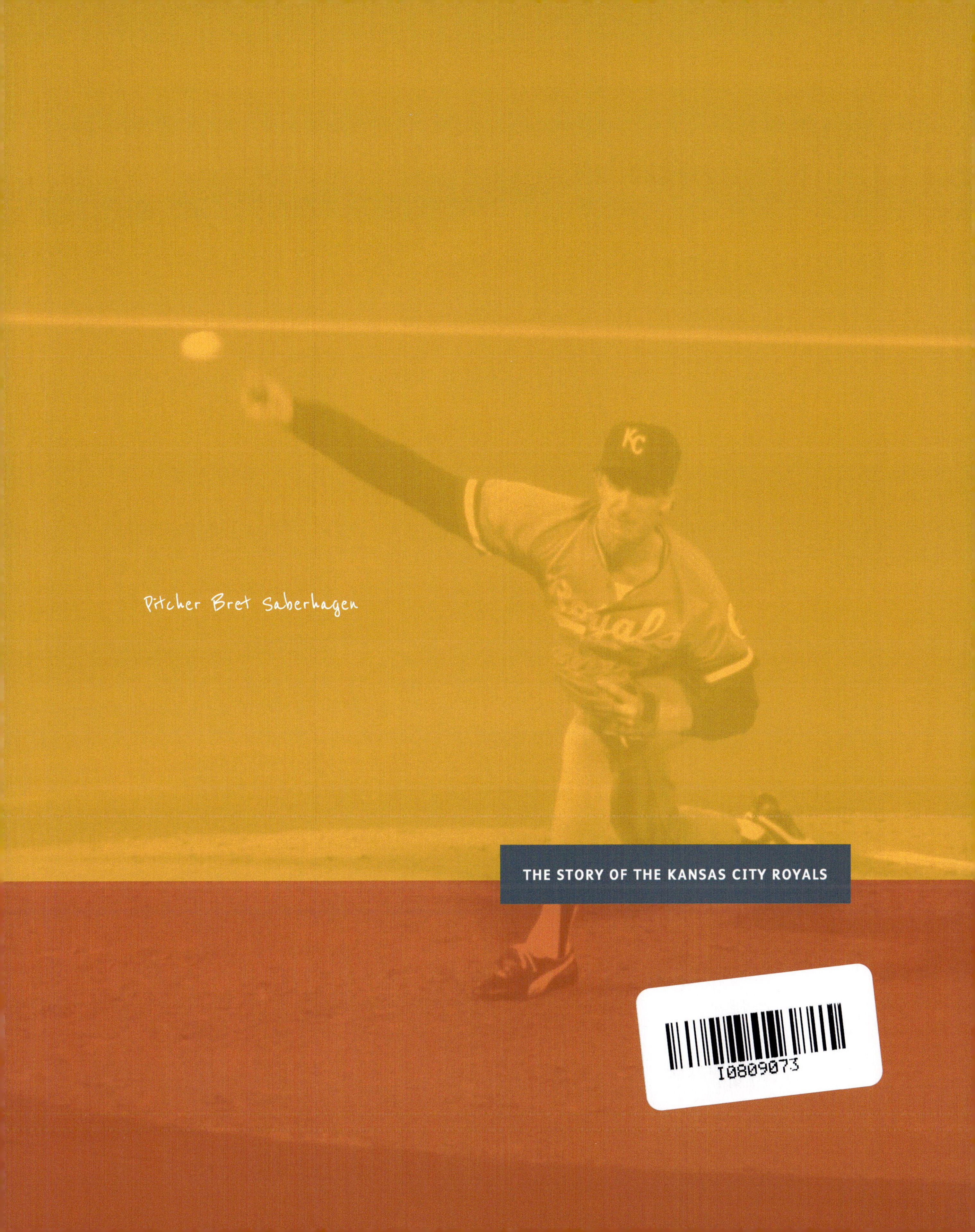

Pitcher Bret Saberhagen

THE STORY OF THE KANSAS CITY ROYALS

Pitcher Michael Wacha

THE STORY OF THE

KANSAS CITY ROYALS

JOE TISCHLER

Outfielder Willie Wilson

CREATIVE SPORTS

CREATIVE EDUCATION / CREATIVE PAPERBACKS

Published by Creative Education and Creative Paperbacks
P.O. Box 227, Mankato, Minnesota 56002
Creative Education and Creative Paperbacks are imprints of
The Creative Company
www.thecreativecompany.us

Book Design by Wyeth Morgan
Art direction by Blue Design (www.bluedes.com)

Images by Alamy Stock Photo/McClatchy-Tribune, 29; Getty Images/B Bennett, 9, 10, Bernstein Associates, cover, 10, Bettmann, 26-27, Daniel Shirey, 30, 31, Ed Zurga, 7 (top, left), Erick W. Rasco, cover, Focus On Sport, 6 (top, right), 15, 18, Jamie Squire, 6 (top, left), 6 (bottom, left), Jeff Carlick, 7 (bottom, right), Joe Robbins/Icon Sportswire, 19, John Williamson, 7 (top, right), Jonathan Daniel, 7 (bottom, left), Josh Umphrey, 22-23, Louis Requena, 12, Mark Cunningham, 25, Nick Cammett/Diamond Images, 2, Otto Greule Jr, 16, Rich Pilling, 1, 6 (bottom, right), 20, Ron Vesely, 3; public domain, 4-5, 32; Shutterstock/f11photo, 11

Library of Congress Cataloging-in-Publication Data
Names: Tischler, Joe author
Title: The story of the Kansas City Royals / by Joe Tischler.
Description: Mankato, Minnesota : Creative Education and Creative Paperbacks, [2026] | Series: Creative sports. Major League baseball | Includes index. | Audience: Ages 8-12 | Audience: Grades 4-6 | Summary: "Discover the Kansas City Royals' thrilling journey as they rose from an expansion team to World Series champions, featuring legendary players, pivotal moments, and the Major League Baseball team's enduring resilience and determination. Written for middle-grade readers. Includes table of contents, sidebars, and index"– Provided by publisher.
Identifiers: LCCN 2025020689 (print) | LCCN 2025020690 (ebook) | ISBN 9798895810958 library binding | ISBN 9798896800484 paperback | ISBN 9798895812211 ebook
Subjects: LCSH: Kansas City Royals (Baseball team)–History–Juvenile literature | Baseball–Missouri–Kansas City–History, Local–Juvenile literature
Classification: LCC GV875.K3 T58 2026 (print) | LCC GV875.K3 (ebook) | DDC 796.357/6409778411–dc23/eng/20250613
LC record available at https://lccn.loc.gov/2025020689
LC ebook record available at https://lccn.loc.gov/2025020690

Printed in the United States

Pitcher Dan Quisenberry

OTIS

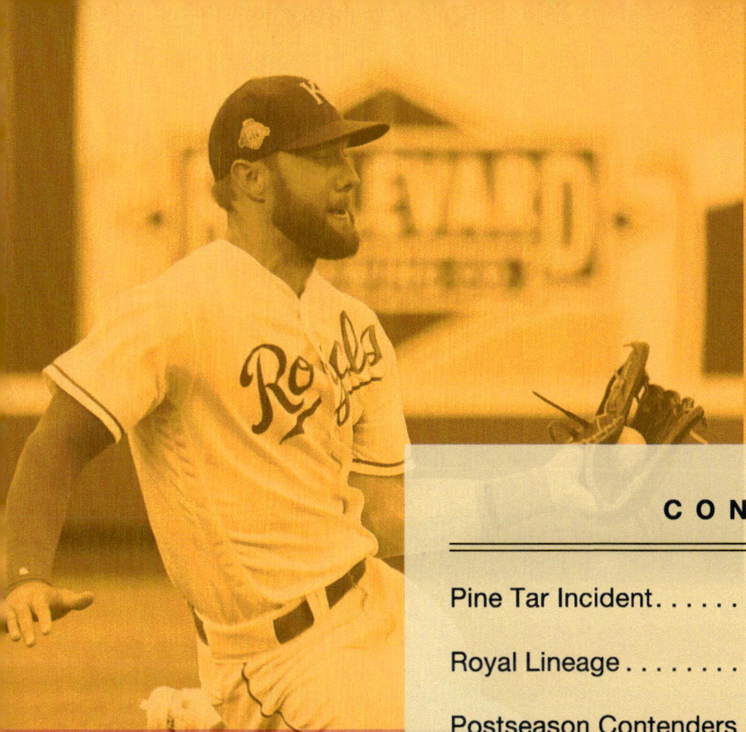

CONTENTS

EXTRA INNINGS

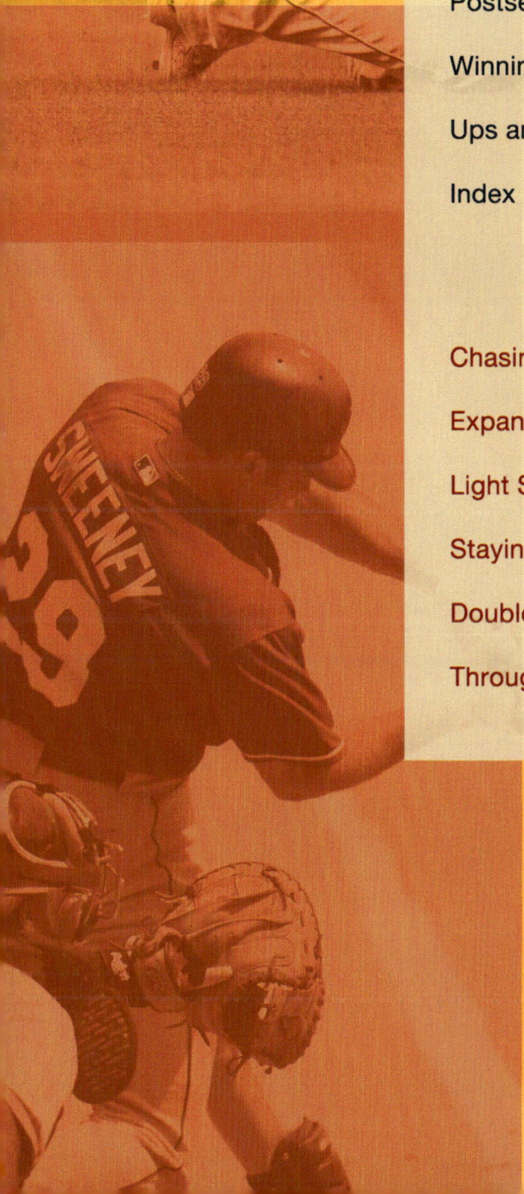

PINE TAR INCIDENT

Despite playing in different divisions, the Kansas City Royals and the New York Yankees were very familiar with each other. From 1976 to 1980, the two teams met in the American League Championship Series (ALCS) four times. The Yankees won the first three times (1976–78) and the Royals won the last playoff meeting (1980).

In 1983, Kansas City and New York met for an important game at Yankee Stadium. Both teams were in the hunt for their respective division titles. On July 24, the Royals were just two games behind the Chicago White Sox for the American League (AL) West lead. The Yankees, meanwhile, were only two games behind the Toronto Blue Jays in the AL East.

On this day, the two teams each scored one run in the second inning. The Royals took a 3–1 lead in the sixth on a run-producing triple from Don Slaught. The Yankees took the lead in the bottom of the sixth with three runs. Don Baylor drove in two runs with a triple. Dave Winfield drove in another with a single.

Third baseman George Brett

KANSAS CITY ROYALS

EXTRA INNINGS

GEORGE BRETT
THIRD BASEMAN/FIRST BASEMAN
ROYALS SEASONS: 1973–93
HEIGHT: 6-FOOT-0
WEIGHT: 185 POUNDS
KEY STATS: 1999 HALL OF FAME INDUCTEE, 1980 AL MVP, 13X ALL-STAR, 3X BATTING CHAMPION

CHASING .400

The last player in MLB history to bat over .400 was Ted Williams. The Boston Red Sox slugger did it in 1941. In 1980, George Brett came close to it. He started the season out slow. He hit only .259 in the first month of the season. He improved in May and hit .329 to raise his average over .300. Brett missed several weeks in June and July due to injury. When he returned, he had hits in 17 of 29 at-bats. He had five hits in Milwaukee on August 26. That raised his average to .407. He was still at .400 on September 19. But he went hitless the next day. His average fell to .396. He finished at .390. Brett was named AL Most Valuable Player (MVP).

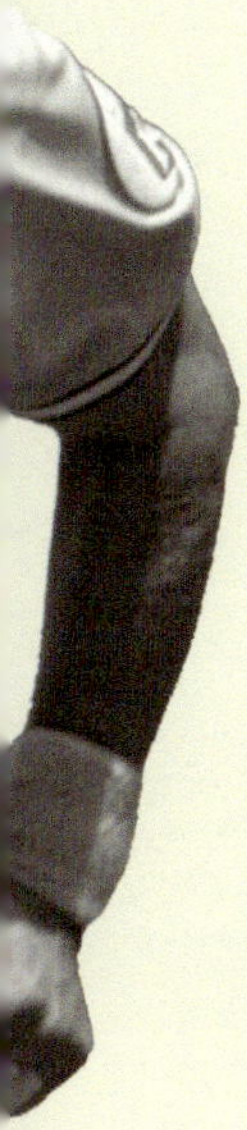

Kansas City Skyline

The Yankees maintained their 4–3 lead going into the ninth inning. The first two Kansas City batters were retired. U. L. Washington kept the game alive for the Royals with a single to center field. Future Hall of Famer closer Rich "Goose" Gossage came on relief for the Yankees. He was tasked with getting out another future Hall of Famer in Royals' third baseman George Brett. On the second pitch of the at-bat, Brett launched a shot well over the right-field wall for a two-run home run. The Royals now led 5–4.

As Brett crossed home plate, Yankees manager Billy Martin came out from the dugout. He requested that home plate umpire Tim McClelland inspect Brett's bat. He thought there was too much pine tar on it. A Major League Baseball (MLB) rule stated that "a bat may not be covered by such a substance more than 18 inches from the tip of the handle." McClelland and the rest of the umpiring crew measured Brett's bat on the width of home plate. They ruled that the pine tar, indeed, exceeded the amount allowed by the rule. McClelland looked at the Royals dugout, pointed at Brett with the bat, and ruled him out. The Yankees won the game, 4–3.

Brett went ballistic. He charged out of the dugout. He had to be restrained by several teammates and coaches. The Royals protested the game.

Four days later, AL president Lee MacPhail upheld the protest. He claimed that the pine tar did not create an unfair advantage. He restored Brett's home run. MacPhail ordered the game to be picked up from that point.

The resumption of the game occurred August 18. Both teams had a scheduled off day. Brett did not take part. He was ejected for his outburst. Royals closer Dan Quisenberry retired the Yankees in order in the bottom of the ninth. The Royals won the game, 5–4.

ROYAL LINEAGE

Before Brett and the Royals ruled Kansas City, an MLB franchise had already called Kansas City home. The Athletics moved there from Philadelphia, Pennsylvania in 1955. The team had little success in its new home. It posted losing records in all 13 seasons it spent there. The team moved to Oakland, California, after the 1967 season.

The move enraged Missouri senator Stuart Symington. He was one of the U.S. Senate's most influential members. He threatened to introduce a bill that would change the structure of big-league baseball. MLB got the message. It was already planning a major expansion that would add two teams to both the AL and National League (NL). One franchise went to Kansas City. It would be part of the new AL West Division. A 1968 name-the-team contest resulted in the choice of "Royals." A yearly livestock show held in Kansas City was known as American Royal.

The Kansas City Royals began play in 1969. They finished the season with a 69–93 record. It was the best mark of the four new teams. One reason was

Left fielder Lou Piniella

left fielder Lou Piniella. His .282 batting average helped earn him AL Rookie of the Year honors. The team slipped to 65–97 in 1970. But the next year, Kansas City enjoyed its first winning season. Its 85–76 mark was second in the AL West.

The team slipped below .500 in 1972. The 1973 season brought a new home and a new franchise player. The club opened Royals Stadium (now Kauffman Stadium). During the season, they called up 20-year-old third baseman George Brett. He would eventually exceed the wildest expectations of Royals management and fans. The team finished 88–74. It was just six games behind the division-winning Athletics.

Within a few years, Brett helped the Royals charge to the top of the AL West. In 1976, he won his first AL batting crown. The Royals won their first division title. But they fell to the Yankees in the ALCS. Kansas City won a franchise-best 102 games in 1977. But, again, it fell to the Yankees in the ALCS.

The same story played out the following year. For the third straight season, the Royals won the AL West. But once again, they lost to the Yankees in the playoffs. Players tried to put a positive spin on the experience. "We didn't look at losing to the Yankees as a big defeat," said second baseman Frank White. "We looked at it as a steppingstone to the future." A brighter future was put on hold in 1979. The Royals finished three games behind the California Angels and out of the playoffs.

EXTRA INNINGS

EXPANSION SUCCESS

In MLB, an expansion team is classified as a team that began their franchise after the 1960 season. There were 16 teams in MLB that season. Fourteen teams have since joined the big leagues, seven in both the AL and NL. Within the first decade of each expansion team's existence, no other team had a better start to their history in the AL than the Kansas City Royals. In 1971, Kansas City recorded its first winning season in only their third season. By 1976, the Royals started a three-year stretch of division championships. Over their first 10 seasons, the Royals had six winning seasons and three playoff appearances.

EXTRA INNINGS

BRET SABERHAGEN
PITCHER
ROYALS SEASONS: 1984–91
HEIGHT: 6-FOOT-1
WEIGHT: 160 POUNDS
KEY STATS: 2X CY YOUNG AWARD, 1985 WORLD SERIES MVP, 3X ALL-STAR, GOLD GLOVE

LIGHT SABER

Bret Saberhagen was not taken until the 19th round of the 1982 MLB Draft. He appeared in his first MLB game on April 4, 1984. He was just 19 years old. The youngster went on to compile a respectable 10–11 record. The following season, he doubled his win total to 20. He won the first of his two AL Cy Young Awards. In the 1985 World Series, Saberhagen threw two complete games. That included a Game 7 shutout to win the World Series. He was named series MVP. He capped his Kansas City career with a no-hitter in 1991. As of 2024, no other Royals pitcher has achieved that feat since.

POSTSEASON CONTENDERS

The Royals finished the 1980 season 97–65. They won the AL West. Who else would they meet in the ALCS but the Yankees. Excellent pitching earned Kansas City wins in the first two games. In Game 3 at Yankee Stadium, New York held a 2–1 lead in the seventh inning. Brett came to bat with two on and two out. He blasted a homer into the upper deck of the outfield stands. "I remember the crack of the bat," said New York pitcher Goose Gossage. "It was like nothing I had ever heard before. I will never forget that crack." The Royals won 4–2 and advanced to their first World Series.

There, they met the Philadelphia Phillies. Kansas City lost the first two games in Philadelphia. The next three games were in Kansas City. The Royals won Games 3 and 4 to tie the series. They led Game 5, 3–2, in the ninth inning. But the Phillies scored twice in the inning. They took a 3–2 series lead back to Philadelphia. The Phillies won Game 6 and captured the title.

The Royals sputtered at the beginning of the 1981 season. They lost 30 of their first 50 games. Then a strike halted the season for several weeks. When play resumed, MLB changed the playoff format. Whoever led the division when the strike started qualified for the playoffs. Whoever won the division when the season resumed would also qualify. The Royals took advantage of this new format. They went 30–23. That gave them the best AL West record after the strike. The Royals met Oakland in the AL Division Series (ALDS). But the Athletics swept the series in three games.

Catcher Darrell Porter

Kansas City finished 90–72 in 1982. But it missed the playoffs. The team fell below .500 the following season. After the 1983 season, four players pleaded guilty to drug charges. They served jail time and were suspended from the league.

The team's 1984 roster featured several new names. One was rookie pitcher Bret Saberhagen. His pinpoint accuracy and surprising maturity earned him a spot in the Royals' starting rotation. Saberhagen helped lead Kansas City back to the top of the division. But the Detroit Tigers powered past the Royals in the playoffs.

Catcher Salvador Pérez

EXTRA INNINGS

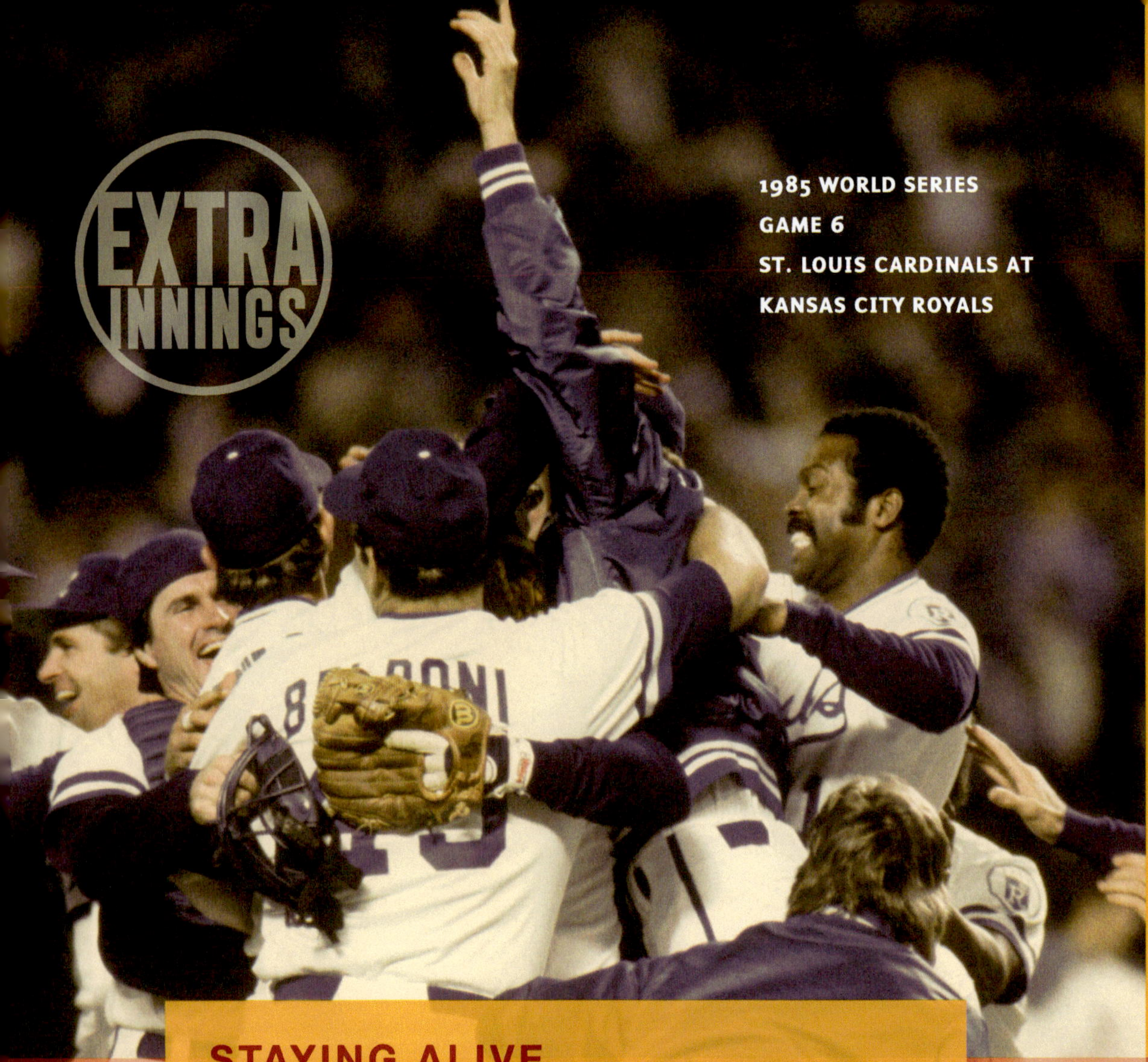

1985 WORLD SERIES
GAME 6
ST. LOUIS CARDINALS AT
KANSAS CITY ROYALS

STAYING ALIVE

The Cardinals led 1–0 going into the bottom of the ninth inning. A win and they would be world champions. The Royals needed to score at least one run to extend the game. Pitching for St. Louis was rookie Todd Worrell. Leading off for Kansas City was pinch-hitter Jorge Orta. Orta chopped a bouncer to first baseman Jack Clark. He tossed the ball to the covering Worrell at first base. The ball appeared to get there before Orta crossed the base. First base umpire Don Denkinger called Orta safe. Television replays showed Worrell's foot on the base with possession of the ball before Orta arrived. Later in the inning, Dane Iorg delivered a two-run single that gave the Royals the win. Kansas City won again the next night to claim their first world title.

WINNING IT ALL

Many Royals players enjoyed individual success in 1985. None was better than Saberhagen, who won 20 games. "I was always amazed not only by the velocity of his fastball, but by the command of his fastball," fellow pitcher Mark Gubicza later recalled. The Royals returned to the postseason. The League Championship Series changed from a best-of-five format to a best-of-seven prior to the 1985 season. The Royals took advantage of this. In the ALCS against the Toronto Blue Jays, Kansas City fell behind, three games to one. In previous years, Toronto would have advanced to the World Series. Kansas City won Game 5 at home. Then it took Games 6 and 7 at Toronto. The Royals were back in the World Series.

Kansas City played the St. Louis Cardinals in the World Series. It was nicknamed the "I-70 Series." Interstate 70 links the two Missouri cities. The Cardinals were heavily favored. They had already won 101 games that year. The Royals had 10 fewer wins.

Like in the ALCS, the Royals fell behind, three games to one. They needed to win three straight games to claim their first world championship. Kansas City stayed alive with a 6–1 win in Game 5 in St. Louis. The Royals used a miracle, a blown call by an umpire, to win Game 6, 2–1. For Game 7, the Royals had their ace on the mound in Saberhagen. Still stunned from what happened the previous night, St. Louis only mustered five hits off Saberhagen. He threw a complete-game shutout. The Royals cruised to an 11–0 win. They were world champions for the first time!

The jubilation of the 1985 championship faded into a disappointing 1986 season. The Royals slipped to 76–86. That season started one of the

KC

Shortstop Ángel Berroa

longest playoff droughts in MLB history, but the slide was not immediately obvious. Kansas City posted winning marks the next three seasons. But each time, they fell short of the playoffs. They came closest in 1987. Steve Balboni, George Brett, and outfielders Bo Jackson and Danny Tartabull each hit at least 22 home runs that year. But they finished two games behind the Minnesota Twins in the AL West.

At the end of the 1992 season, Brett joined the 3,000-hits club. But his offensive production was starting to wane. The following season, the Royals put together an 84–78 record. Afterward, Brett announced his retirement. "I could have played another year, but I would have been playing for the money," he said. "Baseball deserves better than that."

In 1994, MLB implemented a three-division format in each league. Kansas City became part of the AL Central Division. By early August, the Royals were locked in a tight battle with the Chicago White Sox and Cleveland Indians for the top spot. But a players' strike canceled the remainder of the season. Designated hitter Bob Hamelin hit 24 home runs and was named AL Rookie of the Year. Pitcher David Cone won 16 games and the AL Cy Young Award.

UPS AND DOWNS

Eight straight losing seasons followed. The low point came in 2002 when the Royals lost 100 games for the first time in franchise history. New manager Tony Peña brought optimism in 2003. The team won its first nine games of the season. Kansas City led the AL Central for a good portion of the

Outfielder David DeJesus

KC
Royals

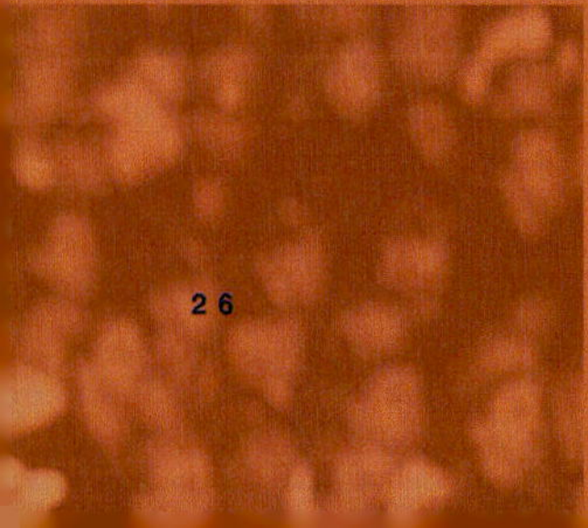

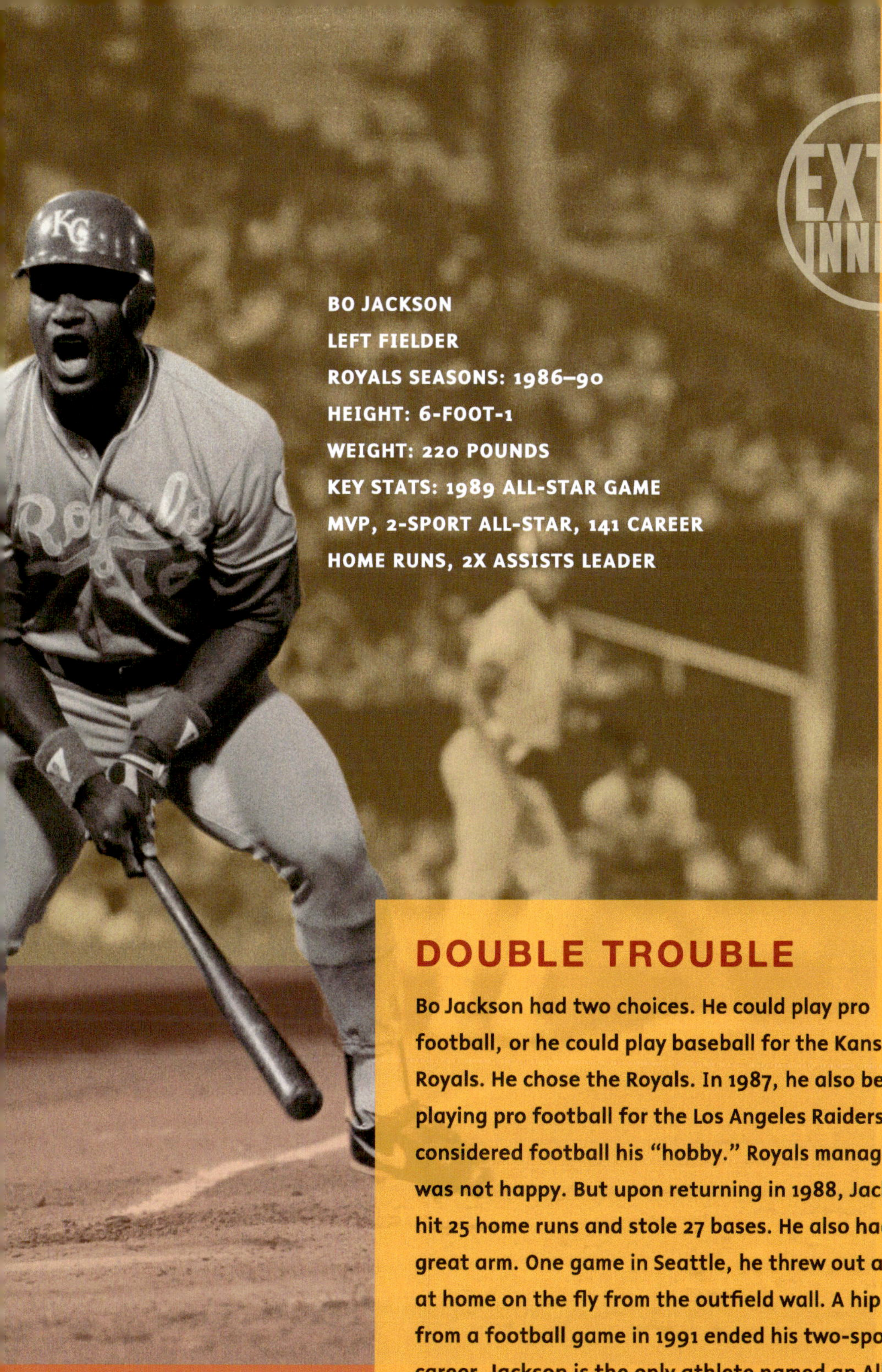

EXTRA INNINGS

BO JACKSON
LEFT FIELDER
ROYALS SEASONS: 1986–90
HEIGHT: 6-FOOT-1
WEIGHT: 220 POUNDS
KEY STATS: 1989 ALL-STAR GAME MVP, 2-SPORT ALL-STAR, 141 CAREER HOME RUNS, 2X ASSISTS LEADER

DOUBLE TROUBLE

Bo Jackson had two choices. He could play pro football, or he could play baseball for the Kansas City Royals. He chose the Royals. In 1987, he also began playing pro football for the Los Angeles Raiders. He considered football his "hobby." Royals management was not happy. But upon returning in 1988, Jackson hit 25 home runs and stole 27 bases. He also had a great arm. One game in Seattle, he threw out a runner at home on the fly from the outfield wall. A hip injury from a football game in 1991 ended his two-sport career. Jackson is the only athlete named an All-Star in both pro baseball and pro football.

season. Shortstop Ángel Berroa was named AL Rookie of the Year. But it started to slide in late August. It finished 83–79, seven games behind Minnesota.

The Royals were back to losing in 2004. It was the start of three straight 100-loss seasons. They lost 106 games in 2005. Despite all of their struggles, the Royals produced young star players. One was pitcher Zack Greinke. In 2009, he won 16 games and led MLB with a 2.16 earned run average (ERA). He won the AL Cy Young Award.

The Royals ended up at the bottom of the division again in 2010. The team traded Greinke. General manager Dayton Moore promised to rebuild. "We expect to be competitive next year," he said. "We're still working to improve our baseball team."

The team finally found success in 2013. For the first time in a decade, Kansas City posted a winning record. In 2014, the Royals finished a close second in the AL Central. Their record was good enough for a spot in the Wild Card game. It marked their first postseason appearance in 29 years. The Royals trailed Oakland 7–3 in the eighth inning. They stormed back to tie the game to send it to extra innings. In the 12th, the Royals scored twice, including a game-winning run-producing hit from catcher Salvador Pérez for the 9–8 win. The Royals kept that momentum going. They swept the Los Angeles Angels of Anaheim in the ALDS. They then swept the Baltimore Orioles in the ALCS.

Kansas City took their perfect postseason record into the World Series against the San Francisco Giants, another Wild Card team. The series went the full seven games. In the final game, San Francisco held a 3–2 lead going into the bottom of the ninth inning. With two outs, Kansas City left fielder Alex Gordon singled. The ball was misplayed. Gordon raced around the bases. He was stopped at third base. The next batter popped out. The game was over.

The Royals topped the AL Central in 2015. It marked their first division title in 30 years. They continued their postseason dominance. They beat the Houston Astros in the ALDS in five games. Then they topped Toronto in the ALCS in six

EXTRA INNINGS

SALVADOR PÉREZ
CATCHER/FIRST BASEMAN
ROYALS SEASONS: 2011–PRESENT
HEIGHT: 6-FOOT-3
WEIGHT: 255 POUNDS
KEY STATS: 2015 WORLD SERIES MVP, 9X ALL-STAR, 5X GOLD GLOVE, 5X SILVER SLUGGER

THROUGH IT ALL

Salvador Pérez has seen plenty of highs and lows during his tenure playing for the Kansas City Royals. Within the first five years with the team, the Royals reached two World Series. In the 2015 World Series, Pérez hit .364 over the five games. He was named series MVP. He has also been a part of many losses. Three times, the Royals have lost at least 100 games. No matter how the team is playing, Pérez is always giving his best. He is a nine-time All-Star. He has won five Gold Glove and Silver Slugger awards. Those are awarded to the best fielder and hitter at each position. Pérez holds the single-season MLB record for home runs as a catcher. He launched 48 of them in 2021.

Royals

Second baseman Jonathan India

games. The Royals were back in the World Series. They took on the New York Mets. Kansas City led three games to one. In Game 5, the Mets led 2–0 going to the ninth inning. Royals first baseman Eric Hosmer drove in a run with a double. Hosmer later scored the tying run to send the game into extra innings. It remained tied until the 12th inning. The Royals scored five runs. The big shot coming off the bat of Lorenzo Cain delivered a bases-clearing double. Royals closer Wade Davis struck out the side in the bottom of the 12th. The Royals were champions!

Kansas City soon stumbled again. It lost over 100 games in 2018, 2019, and 2023. They had a stunning turnaround in 2024. Led by star shortstop Bobby Witt Jr., the Royals went from 56 wins in 2023 to 86 in 2024. Witt Jr. was runner-up in AL MVP voting. He led MLB with a .332 batting average. He belted 32 home runs and drove in 109 runs. The Royals made the postseason as a Wild Card. They swept Baltimore in the AL Wild Card Series. But they fell to the Yankees in the ALDS.

Kansas City has witnessed some exciting baseball since the Royals' debut in 1969. Their history includes tight postseason battles, two World Series titles, and legendary players. Royals fans remain confident that their team will soon seize the crown again.

Relief Pitcher Carlos Estévez

INDEX